WIN TER CRA NES

POEMS

CHRIS BANKS

MISFIT

ECW Press

Published by ECW Press
2120 Queen Street East, Suite 200, Toronto, Ontario, Canada M4E 1E2
416-694-3348 / info@ecwpress.com

Library and Archives Canada Cataloguing in Publication

Banks, Chris, 1970-
Winter cranes / Chris Banks.

Poems.
ISBN 978-1-77041-018-3
Also issued as: 978-1-77090-104-9 (PDF); 978-1-77090-103-2 (EPUB)

I. Title.

PS8553.A564W56 2011   C811'.6   C2011-902940-5

Editor for the press: Michael Holmes / a misFit book
Cover design: David Gee
Text design: Tania Craan
Typesetting: Mary Bowness
Printing: Coach House Printing 1 2 3 4 5

The publication of *Winter Cranes* has been generously supported by the Canada Council for the Arts, which last year invested $20.1 million in writing and publishing throughout Canada, by the Ontario Arts Council, by the Government of Ontario through Ontario Book Publishing Tax Credit, by the OMDC Book Fund, an initiative of the Ontario Media Development Corporation, and by the Government of Canada through the Canada Book Fund.

  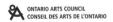

PRINTED AND BOUND IN CANADA

FOR TERESA, HANNAH AND NOAH

Thanks Fred!
Nice to meet you!
Chris Banks

CONTENTS

I

II

III

I hide behind simple things so you'll find me;
if you don't find me, you'll find the things,
you'll touch what my hand has touched,
our hand-prints will merge.

Yannis Ritsos from "The Meaning of Simplicity"

I

Darkening

•

The simple joy of riding with good friends
in a car coming back from a barn dance
on the edge of a great lake in mid-March,
driving through falling snow on blizzarding
country roads, past farms, silos, cattle barns
recessed in deep shadows as *Stand By Me*
spills from the radio. But on that night
our car hit black ice and skittered across
the road's slick surface like a water bug
— twenty-odd yards — before coming to rest
in a snowbank beside a farmer's house.
A man appeared out of the dark, walking
down his laneway. He asked if anyone
was hurt. Are you okay? Seeing the car
was undamaged, he said he could tow it
out with his tractor. I remember that
night walking up the road, a hundred yards
or more, in the moonless dark, without so
much as a flare or a flashlight to wave down
passing cars, wondering why my friends
and I had survived the crash. Wondering
why I was not dead. I can still see myself
standing impatiently, wind barreling
across fields, over snow fences, the cold
licking raw the flesh beneath my jacket,
trying to hail the drivers of three cars
not bothering to stop, not quite certain
whether they saw a figure half-glimpsed
in the helixing snow at that late hour,
a messenger risen up from the ground,
to warn them of some impending hazard
until too late they found an old tractor

upon the road. And what I remember
of that night will not call back anyone
from the past. Not the vehicles swerving
to carve a wide groove in a winter field
crusted with thin ice and eddying snow.
Not the farmer on the tractor cursing,
his breath rising, a white scar, mixing in
plumes of diesel smoke in the chilly air.
Not even my younger self, who I see
standing roadside like an apparition
turning his body to stare back down
the dark hallway of a moment ago.

Exodus

•

The wind in the white birches
moves across the valley's floor,
the farms, the fields, the orchards
where fruit pickers long gone
work each new harvest season
singing laments and drinking
rum in the cool evenings
of cheap roadside motel rooms.
It rushes past the villages
and townships, the stone fences,
the barbed wire, as if looking
for its name etched, chiseled
among white cemeteries
with historical bronze plaques
beside gas stations for sale,
or underneath small bridges
in the storyless silence
of creeks and rivers flowing
through generations of lives
built along their muddy banks.
Wending through every shape
— ravines, gorges, and forests —
it moves deeply inside even us,
wanting to lie in our bodies,
and not keep moving, looking
always for a place to rest.

Winter Cranes

•

My wife saw birds pass over the frozen pond
and wondered aloud if they were cranes,
desiring proof of their corporeal existence
to mark them as either a tangible reality
or a fantasy born of some lack in our lives.
Their wings beat exultantly, blossoming,
a wild spume of feathers backlit by morning sun
so they looked like more than just creatures
but symbols ferried from myth or poetry
to satisfy my wife's wishes or my need to place
a few lines down upon the blank sheet
of this morning's latest offering of snow.
I said they were only herons. The same ones
from last summer come back a little early,
guided by an instinct, a faint signal, hard-wired
in their brains to the earth's magnetic fields
allowing them to navigate their way here
each year to stand like sentries, silhouettes
against the pond's grey light, if only to teach us
how even patience can be a kind of violence.
"I want them to be cranes," my wife said again,
a little more forcefully this time, so her words
were now a truth or a sacrament of experience
fully grasped, making us hungry for the dynasties
of the past we believe such birds emerge from
like after-images of a dream only now recalled.
"I wish they were cranes too," I said, watching
the pair descending towards the farthest end
of the pond where the ice was the thinnest,
the city hardening its shell in the background,
still waiting for the winter storms to come.

Locations

•

Meadowlark, sweetgrass, milkweed bursting like cotton-fluff:
    all of nature's excesses burgeoning in a vacant lot
bounded on one side by a suburb full of blasé dot-com-ers,
    vassals of the new economy, who drive expensive suvs
and marinate their lawns in chemicals, and on the other side
    a meat factory whose workers sit on little picnic benches
and smoke in the summer sunshine while on lunch break

beside tiny purple flowers whose name I have forgotten
    and which are probably weeds anyway. Nearby,
a little boy in a Batman mask stands at the end of his street
    waving at strangers as a river of cars washes by.
Young mothers push infants in strollers, exchange numbers,
    sipping chai lattes, while even the elderly are out
teetering on sidewalks in small groups of two or three

(they hold onto each other like survivors of a small war zone).
    Each step is a battle they wage with their bodies
so full as they are of old griefs and consolations. Little birds
    strafe the air. Their mellifluous voices breezing past
a young blind man out walking with his shirt off — the tick tick
    of his white cane on the cement taking a constant
measure of his contentment. An army of lawn mowers

sound warnings to civilization in the distance. Back across
    the road, who is crouching in the middle of the lot
deep inside the wild phlox and red clover, staring through
    the tall grasses at the black gates to the underworld?
What has he found among the anthills, the grasshoppers,
    the commercial real estate sign, but a no man's land —
one that needs to be itemized, one leaf, one rock, at a time.

Rome

•

Once I found myself in a strange and eternal city
      where saints and angels looked down upon me
from every building. A city built on immortality;
      narrow cobblestone streets and marble palazzos
quarried from myth and history and Italian hills.
      I had been drinking red wine and feeling sorry
for my luck, sitting with new companions, two
      Irish men and a tall American girl, all of them

chattering while I sulked, mourning the loss of
      three days' travel time, after I was found without
a metro ticket at Stazione Termini, and promptly
      fined a hundred thousand lire by a police officer.
I was twenty-six years old, seated on the Spanish
      Steps, right across from the house where Keats
lay suffering on his deathbed for almost a month
      coughing up at times a full pint of blood a day,

while his friend Severn, the painter, mopped up
      a sweat clinging like beaded ice to his cheeks
and played for him an arrangement of Haydn's
      symphonies on a rented piano until one night
he died. His life consumed too soon, Keats went
      into whatever knowing death is, leaving behind
the smoking noun of his name, abandoning it
      to ill fame and fate. But at the time, I was not

thinking of poetry, or the high price Keats paid
      at his journey's end. I was a foolish young man
thinking of myself, and how I would have to stop
      my trip without having seen the Alps. I knew

nothing about transcendence. Only the wish to be
    elsewhere. I was not thinking about that famous
young man who had come to that city before me
    dreaming of faraway lands he would never see.

For Adam

Nothing is more lost or imagined
than the libraries of classical antiquity
vanished in flood, in fires, to pillagers

or to the slow sear of age eating page
after page until bookshelves sat empty.
None are left apart from Herculaneum,

playground retreat for the Roman elite,
but it took a massive volcanic eruption
to ensure two thousand papyrus scrolls

carbonized instantly after the heat-blast,
the earth-spatter and the hot lava flows
went through the city like a wave of fire.

And what books could they possibly be?
Poems by Sappho? Plays by Sophocles?
Aristotle's lost second book of poetics?

We may not know since early excavators
sunk shafts and dug underground tunnels
entering the Villa of the Papyri in gondolas

only to find what they thought were torches
scattered on the floor and striking a match
burned — what? The opus of Epicurus?

Livy's *History of Rome*? And like the dead
whose work they were destroying forever
they kindled words to light the way ahead.

The Late Great Encyclopedia Men

•

They stand at the entrance of a house
unable to lift a finger to ring the bell

knowing they have joined the late,
great ranks of salesmen who haunt

airport lounges and hotel bars
telling stories of how they too once

carved out a territory for themselves
like Romulus and Remus, an empire

of neon lights and red clay dirt farms.
But had they lived in that other time

their lives would be worth the same,
no more than the scattered leaves

rattling under a car's dusty wheels
as they go to and from destinations

they can't even recall week to week
which is why they stand so motionless,

hesitating on someone's front stoop,
not daring to disturb the neighbourhood,

watching the faint shadows they cast
on the sidewalks in the early evenings.

How insubstantial they look walking
already forgotten in the coming dusk.

Riverland

•

A community runs through it, the sign
says beside the housing development,
painting images of fly-fishermen
in hip waders, knee-deep in currents
pulling out trout, one-handed, while
happily waving at men and women
mowing lawns, grilling filet mignon
on backyard hibachis. Such illusions
conjured up by a marketing whiz kid
to sell condos to retirees, cavernous
houses, small fortresses, to families.
Already past the fields of goldenrod,
chicory, butter and eggs, wild lupines,
there are wooden posts sticking out in
all directions with flags of orange tape
to mark off where the new boundaries
between subdivisions and wilderness
have been drawn in the indivisible air.
Riverland this is, presumably, for now —
but it runs through erector-set towers
carrying power lines from one suburb
to the next and soon those populations
on the horizon will move to these banks
and this river will inscribe its pattern
inside the lines of a city planner's map
so people may live the uncommon life
that's been promised to us for so long now
it's impossible not to see the rows
of replica homes standing on its shores,
their blank faces gazing upon its surface,
and never, not once, feel it leaving us.

The Griffon

Unfathomed, it sleeps
at the bottom of Lake Michigan,
the first ship to sail the upper Great Lakes,
after mysteriously vanishing on
its maiden voyage in 1679
with its six-man skeleton crew
and a valuable freight of furs,
so we are forced to improvise a myth
around this grail of shipwrecks,
an antiquarian's water-logged dream,
imagining its wooden spars
splintering in the lake's graveyard,
squeezed by black bellows,
its wet hafts, mud-struck beams
battered by limestone, shale,
sandstone, halite, gypsum — its hull
revised, deranged, unmade,
until it is no longer a lost ship,
but a tangle of rotting planks,
the wreckage of a forgotten age
treasure hunters trawl for
in long veils of lime-silt water
as if something both permanent
and real could be salvaged by
a human desire pure enough
to haul what is left of its origins
all the way up to the surface.

Ghosts

•

You begin to practice holding your breath.
Without effort, or air, you pass a minute
surprised your lungs do not beg for release.
A minute and a half passes, and you
slowly feel a bubble of trapped pressure
build and pull itself through the chest's walls.
A deep sea bulwark collapsing. But still
you meditate on a great nothingness
and the panic ceases. The minutes pass.
You wonder how it is that you are alive.
You walk through the city. People stare through you.
You touch a homeless man's shoulder. He gives
nothing away. Only yawns. Blinks twice. Then stares,
blankly. One of you is not there.

Testament

•

Out at the end of the camp's property
sat the government dock where as teens
we stripped off our clothes every summer
to stand shivering, naked and wide-eyed,

led by some inner compulsion beyond
the glow of cottage lights and the waves
lapping the small stones smooth on shore
until they pebbled, broke apart — the bonds

holding matter to matter worried loose
by the sucking ebb of wave upon wave.
Perhaps that was the impulse we felt too
walking down into the lake's black mirror

until we could no longer see ourselves,
sense only the oily waters like myrrh
anoint our bodies in the pure condition
of being momentarily alive and awake.

The moonlight pouring its cold cup of milk
down upon our heads, baptizing us again
in the names of not our fathers, but there,
on those nights, in the names of our youth

as we swam out towards the lake's centre
far from the shore, the unbroken music
of the waves closing around those places
where a moment before we once had been.

Voyages

•

I used to imagine I heard music
along the strand of a great lake

when as a young man I listened
to tired waves cast themselves

upon shore like a siren's spell
once used to summon people

to hull together in a ship's belly
across the wide Atlantic Ocean.

I know my wife's grandparents
made the voyage from Hungary

though to even speak of it brings
tears to her grandmother's eyes

when she thinks of those vessels
I saw from afar when they came

into dock for repairs at shipyards
that have been closed for decades

but employed the fathers of boys
who were in my classes at school,

names scrawled in old notebooks,
where now these fishermen stand

casting nylon lines out on the docks
beside the giant cast-iron moorings

the empty berths falling into ruins.
I am sure they hear that music too,

telling them any day a ship will come
to bear them off to a promised land.

Stacking Cordwood

•

My father believes stacking a woodpile
is an art form like Chinese ink drawing
or High Renaissance painting. It requires
an apprenticeship which lasts a lifetime.
So much of my childhood, I remember,
was spent riding in the back of his truck
through mile after mile of ministry lands
until we came to our crown-appointed lot.
A good half-acre of hardwoods, pure and
precious and uncut. A crowd of species:
white birch, sugar maple, hickory, beech.
Dad started working out from the centre,
felling trees with his almighty chainsaw
until his arms were a fine paste of sweat
and sawdust. A heavy smell of chain oil
clung to our clothing and stung our eyes
while my brother and I worked forever
to pile the wood into the truck's flatbed.
The real work came after returning home
when dad, hefting the blunt end of his axe,
would smash it down onto an iron maul
wedged into a hard knot of wood to split
one stick into two, two sticks into four;
the three of us — dad, my brother, me —
all worked as one to get the wood hewn,
stacked in the basement, before the sky
let down its rain. Even then it would be
months before he would allow it to burn.
Still green, he'd say. It had to be seasoned
until it was dark, grey, dingy as old stone,
cracked in its inner rings. The best wood
for burning is aged, bone dry, and cured.

Each stick or bolt of wood has to be set
against the next in just such a way that
a balance is maintained, like setting type
inside a chase; splits need to be jostled,
twisted, flipped, and aligned for an even
aspect to match the last row with no gaps,
ending with a double criss-crossed stack
to keep the edifice from tumbling down.
You've got a gift, he'd say, examining
my handiwork as I slid the last chunk
of wood into its place on the woodpile,
a fire inside me beginning to blaze.

Fragrance

•

My father sits in the Volkswagen bug
in the driveway of our first house.
I am four years old and listless.
He passes me his pipe and shows me
how to tamp down the tobacco
the way he likes it. "Here," he says,
"this is your job," and I do it,
pinching a little pouch tobacco,
its mixture of cherry and cassis,
between thumb and forefinger,
stuffing it carefully into the bowl
so my father smiles ever so softly,
tousling my bright reddish hair
before lighting his pipe. Sad how
men do not smoke pipes anymore —
except for the old or the very few
who stand outside barber shops.
The aroma is thick and cloying,
like a sealed room that has not
been opened for many decades
after someone you loved always
leaves to go far away. I remember
driving the many miles to town,
my father singing a popular song
on the radio while I tamped down
his tobacco, then closing my eyes,
I let his smoke wash over my face.
Was it only yesterday I caught again
the dark scent of its sweet fragrance?
Nostalgia, whiffing up, curlicuing,
surrounding me still like a room?

Thief

•

I jimmied open the basement window,
rusty hinges swinging slowly inward,
shimmied myself onto the high shelf,
letting my feet drop towards the floor,
before padding stealthily up the stairs
like a five-year-old apprentice thief.
My neighbours were eating breakfast
at a small round table in their kitchen
without ever speaking to one another
or seeing me standing on the stairwell.
I kept my vigil for maybe five minutes,
then left the same way I had come in
without ever thinking of their privacy —
until yesterday when I was cleaning out
the basement, then saw a shaft of light
pour itself through an unlatched window.
It triggered in me a sudden wave of guilt;
or was it simply déjà vu? What passed
passed I always thought, but how else
to explain that sliver of light, and then
a who's who of my memories, breaking
and entering into the story of my life?

Bye Bye Blackbird

Why do I miss the spidery apple trees
and their mottled fruit scattered,
leathery, upon the ground?
The baby carriages, untended,
all lined up against the supermarket.
The young mothers shopping.
The coin collection I shined just to see
the boy in my grandfather's eyes.
The pocket watch he carried
stopped at 11:58, then kept closed
in a desk drawer forever.
The chimes of pinball machines
from June to September.
The worn felt of a pool table
in 1963 when my father won $200
in a single afternoon.
The three blackbirds he picked off
a telephone pole with an air rifle
teaching me to laugh at death and chaos
when I was only five years old.
The clotheslines pegged out in the back alleys
and the smell of the dry cleaners.
Their clam-shell machines pressing out
the folds and the wrinkles,
pleating moment to moment.
The milk bottles left empty
on the front stoop, and these ones
I give back to you now, full.

Improbable

•

Sometime in 1982, two boys are swinging
a cat by its tail, after having burned its ears
and whiskers with a lighter, as if cruelty
was still commonplace and not relegated
to the pages of a history textbook. I am
watching them but I am also watching from here
across the improbable space of thirty years.
This is the illusion time and the human spirit
bring together. What makes the cat cry out
for its own existence and another boy fling
himself off his bike onto the cat's tormentors.
Gratefully, I can see the cat has escaped
into a nearby yard where many years ago
I imagined it turned into dust and dirt.

David
•

There in the backyard
smoking a cigarette
in his red baseball cap
and denim overalls
crowing in a language
not even his family
can parse into words
stands a 23-year-old
autistic man: David.
He walks a platform
his mother uses to pin
the family's washing
to an old clothesline,
smoking the cigarette
while the neighbours
watch him gesturing,
first placing his hands
above his head, then
lowering them quickly,
repeating the motion,
until slowly, carefully,
he shifts his weight,
and lifts up his feet
so if you were to turn
away for an instant
you would miss seeing
him, lighter than air,
rise above the fences.

Cold War

·

Rounding the pathway, I said my prayers
like any twelve-year-old after confession.
Oak palisades lined each side of the street.
Big trees in full leaf wearing rusty colours
like insignias of Fall's surrender. I thought
about the soft cymbals of the falling rain
hitting the sidewalks too. How it dampened
everything I passed — the friendship centre,
the candy store, the dirty garage smelling
of oil pans and used tires — and whether
it was that awful rain that turned bones
into a brittle chalk. Would it be possible
for Soviet soldiers to surround my town
like so many Hollywood films prophesied?
How would planes sneak past the radar base
sitting like a giant modern-white Pantheon
on a cliff face above the iron trestle bridge
trains rattled across on their way out west?
TV preached Star Wars and apocalypse-light
to children who, bequeathed a world
they could not yet begin to fully appreciate,
took refuge by drifting inwardly as I did,
scuffing wet clumps of leaves with my shoes
noticing the mark they left, the impression
of bodies vaporized, there on the sidewalks.

The Desert

•

A man is driving himself to the office
    taking the same route he has taken
every day of his life for the past ten years
    when street signs and intersections
begin to fade and fall back. His wheels
    suddenly lose traction and sink

in loose sand, and when he steps out
    to look for landmarks familiar to him,
he notices his car is already half-buried
    in a wide and permanent desert.
Knowing this day was inevitable,
    the man takes off his suit and tie

and only stops long enough to check
    his car's trunk for the few provisions
he had thought to pack: a box of saltines,
    iodine pills, an astrolabe, a pocket Keats,
before abandoning his car to the vultures
    and the heat and then, seemingly

unconcerned, he begins to pick his way
    towards the dunes. Not glancing back,
knowing he will die alone, without ceremony
    or lasting epitaphs, he places each foot
carefully down upon the shifting sands
    and sets out for his eye's horizon.

"This is not a poem," the smart-dressed man with the slide rule said as we walked across a field full of gold bees nosily excavating pollen from the bursting flowers. Clouds were casting long shadows over distant hills. "I assure you this is a poem," I said, plucking a blade of grass and watching the brittle light eat away at its green interior. "That is nonsense," the young man said. His brow weighed down by too much knowledge, and not enough pure intention. "This is a sentence," he said, "Where is the line?" "The line is here," I said. "It is just a different kind of line." At that moment, birds began to sing and the two of us began to meditate on some deep remembered past, birdsongs rising, and falling, and circling back to the hidden sources we draw our lives from. "There is no such thing as a prose lyric," the middle-aging young man said, measuring with his slide rule a nearby branch to see if he could calculate, in syllables, its material fact. "Poetry is abundance," I told him. "Listen to the river, the birds, and the wind. In that plenitude, that fullness, even Time is suspended." "There is no river, no birds, no wind, and no trees," the man said, touching his fingers to the scarred bark of a large tree. "That is partly true," I said, "These are only innuendoes." Mistakenly, he thought I was making fun of him, and not to be outdone, the man stomped the ground and said, "All is prosody." "All is paraphrase," I calmly reminded him. "But there are no line breaks," he said. "But there are line continuums," I suggested. Finally, becoming more testy, he stammered, "Nothing is happening here!" "Ah, but poetry makes nothing happen," I said quoting Auden back to him which is when he grew silent, started to mutter to himself, and taking his slide rule in hand, fell to the ground and began to measure each blade of grass.

The Garden Maze

•

It was mid-day and I had been moving through the maze for over an hour. No one had been guarding its iron gates. What lay at its center, a classical treasure or a rare special knowledge, was still hidden deep within its walls. Every so often others would push past me going in the wrong direction — men, women, children and the elderly. One man in a linen suit gave me a half-finished bottle of wine. Another gave me a heel of bread. Then someone was playing a harp nearby. Each note fretted the sunlight weaving it through the perfumed air. It was a melody of pure delight. Later the music was drowned out and there was only the sound of locks clicking open and shut, and from far away, clocks striking upon the hour. Loneliness crept into the shadows and hid behind every twisting corner. The hedge walls became more stunted, varicosed with vines, as time began to close around them. I began to feel older and to forget my own name. Only my indiscretions could I still remember. I questioned what right I had to be walking here when I could not dissemble the right path. It began to make no great difference whether I went forward or back. Each way felt barred but still a strange magnetism, an issuing patience, compelled me. At last, I reached the heart of the maze and I saw a desolate figure sitting solitary upon a stone bench in the middle of a marble courtyard. As I approached him, I saw at once why the others had turned around. It was me sitting there. "You better make yourself comfortable," I said. "You are going to be here for a very long while."

I

•

Late yesterday,
the wind began
dusting the yard
for fingerprints.
It could not find
my little daughter
anywhere. The cat
sat in the window
chattering, clawing
at a fat sparrow.
St. Benedict was
said to have seen
the soul of his sister
rise up to heaven
as a dove. The bird
from yesterday
perched on our
neighbour's fence
and sang heartily
"Don't forget me!"
yet was no one
I remember.

II
•

Our bird friend is back.
Its medley of notes
is an occasional song
our cat Zen loves.

He wants nothing
more than to pluck out
the bright red apple
of its ruby heart.

III
●

What are you afraid of
walking along the river
this early morning? Fog

rolling over its surface
like a wispy smoke. Sun
making its arid light

for your passage here.
*Nothing. I'm afraid
of nothing*, the river

says, one apple tree,
a confetti of blossoms,
tiny boats in its stream.

IV

•

I heard for the first time
my daughter's heartbeat
last week at the midwife

appointment. She placed
a wand against my wife's
stomach and it was, yes,

the sound of waves hitting
a reef off the coast of Fiji
but played at double-speed

and from a great distance
as if an old gramophone,
its black lacquered wood,

was lying on white sands
somewhere playing music
at the edges of the world.

V

•

Sun warms the tall reeds.
This hour, a spiderweb

dimples with early light.
I wade into the river

stumbling over smooth
stones. A trout swims out

breaking the still surface
like a soul emerging.

Late Hour

•

Her cries come into my study from the next room
    where she snuffles and mewls like a little animal,
what she is saying lost in the labyrinths of sleep,
    that secondary life. I think of her scrubbed skin
smelling of soft peaches and the nightmares that
    twist her fears into the hurdy-gurdy of baby terrors
as I sit contemplating what lies beneath the hard
    shellac of words, as if I could explain how perfectly
a father loves his children, and how insufficient

    that is to a six-month-old calling for her mother
to nurse her. Later, I will get up from my desk
    to walk quietly down the hall, a man who tells
the truth of his life to strangers — or at least what
    I know as the truth. But tomorrow, I will rise early
from my bed to listen to my daughter half-cooing,
    half-singing to herself, and soon entering her room,
she will remember her need of her father again.
    An inexorable love that sets me above all things.

These are the dog days spent
watching storm-pelted clouds
tick past the tops of houses,
slow-moving barges towing
an old melancholy across
a cold September morning
where little children drag
school-bags along sidewalks
towards playgrounds empty
but for swing sets blossomed
with orange rust, rainwater
pooling under rubber seats.
Bright gouts of leaves, russets,
yellows, and oranges ablaze
send up weak smoke signals
from yards or else all crowd
together in ditches, gutters,
storm drains, avatars of loss
both beautiful and suicidal
to roving packs of teenagers
who wander like a lost tribe
feeling childhood's slaughter
draw near. They trudge past
chewing the word *me* like gum
between them, not wanting
to catch up with those futures
they have already foreseen.
They know the streets belong
to someone else, just as they
they know the keys to the city
were given to their parents,
so they armour themselves

against a cloudy nothingness
they suspect is lurking behind
the façade of streets and houses
suffering the heavy weather
of the present, wearing a look
of boredom they believe to be
pressure-treated, future-proof,
able to withstand what is
always and always ending.

Graffiti

·

A young man is spray-painting graffiti,
writing his name in street calligraphy
no one is meant to recognize at all,
except himself and his urban brethren,
friends and enemies, adolescent boys
with god complexes, permanent markers,
jacked-up attitudes in ripped jeans, T-shirts.
They tag billboard signs, super mailboxes,
boarded-up restaurants, washroom-stall doors,
public schools, shopping malls, city centres.
Tonight this boy stands with spray can in hand
working the longhand scrawl of syllables
and vowels, inscriptions to give meaning
to the buildings populating the night.
Warehouses like tombs or ossuaries
commemorating nothing but hazards.
Each street is empty but for the black cars
resting in moonlight. The lone alley cat
walking between them and the gutters.
This night the boy feels himself dissolving
into the dark, believing he is gone,
he is fleshless, and the world a long dream
without a place for him in its story,
so he must write his own mythology
if only to make real the firmament,
signing his name in every lost place.

Django Reinhardt Plays the Blues

•

With two digits on his left hand,
    the others burned
badly in a gypsy encampment's
    fire, he plays tunes
like a maimed god. Never playing
    the melody straight,
always improvising new notes,
    harmonic textures,
fiddle-schtick and jazz riffs.
    In the Paris clubs
or travelling with the caravans,
    he played his music
the way he heard it. In the mix
    and without caution
while diners drank white wine,
    ate mussels, fried
potatoes, and caroused until dawn.
    No one understood
how such a prodigy could be
    Romani, untrained,
self-taught, but only a nomad
    could make a guitar croon
sweet and lowdown or skip out
    of a sold-out concert hall
to stroll casually under a full moon
    along half-empty streets.
He learned to play the blues
    out in the country air,
from men in striped waistcoats
    and broad-brimmed
hats who lived like vagabonds,
    tinkers on the doorsteps

of Europe's greatest civilizations.
    Women with kiss-curls
in long-flowing dresses cooking
    food on open firepits,
while dogs and brawling children
    played in weedy ditches.
A technique not taught, but lived,
    so whether he played
his guitar for dancing bears or
    jazz-loving Nazis during
WWII to escape the Porajmos,
    it was the same music.
His chromatic solos running
    up and down six strings,
awakening a dreamy melancholy,
    an imaginative lightness
that once heard lifted the spirit
    above the body's reach
as if in the many breaks the violin
    or the piano left him,
he found a passion more than
    melody, an energy
that if you could just hear once
    would sustain your life.

The Only Picture of Hernandez, New Mexico, in the Smithsonian Institute

•

A man and his son driving on Highway 84, a two-lane black-top
thirty miles from Sante Fe, pull over onto the shoulder, noticing
the moon's face poised over the snow-capped Truchas mountains;

the darkness falling over the tree-lined banks of the Rio Chama
flowing down to meet the Rio Grande, the smell of sage, burning
pinion, its woodsy fragrance, rising from the chimneys of houses

in a village sitting beside a church, a graveyard full of white crosses.
He sets up his tripod on the roof of his car. The light is failing him
so he must work quickly, fumbling with lens filters, film holders,

all the variables and unknowns, estimating the moon's luminosity,
exposure times, shutter speeds, while shadows consume the daylight
where the adobe church, a monument, stands illuminated at dusk

glowing from within. The white crosses flush, no longer ornaments
but part of the spirit's nomenclature. Heaven and Earth conjoin
at the back of the man's retina, a cloudbank hovering magisterially

as he snaps the photograph trying to pull back the shutter again,
but the light changes, the impetus fades, and the world is suddenly
only the world again. Weeks later, he improvises in his darkroom

half-tones of feeling, dodging and burning in areas, making the sky
endlessly dark, the sagebrush a mural of silver, the village empty
as in a child's dream. He uses sleight of hand to extract a confession

from the land, teasing out light and darkness so it speaks quietly,
poignantly, like a revelation. Nothing is forever but looking deeply
at the world, as it was made over fifty years ago, through a lens

ministers to man's hope for redemption although none is coming,
for the man who took this picture has gone into those mountains
so completely he has become them. Who knows if a town existed,

or if anyone had ever lived there, until in the darkness of his room
he placed the moon to look over it, light moving through the crosses,
making us believe, if for a time, it is possible to outlast the night.

The Visitation

•

Driving I follow the highway's wet pavement
past the bronze hills and the unkempt fields,
the dirty truckstops and the all night diners,

fuelled by an inner insistence that carefully
clings to the way the road unravels its length
one mile at a time through the countryside

until finally I hit upon the limits of a town,
its name written in rust above the iron gates
I pass through as if they had been left open

for my arrival. Like someone half-expected
me to find this place many, many years ago
and it was only now I had taken the journey,

driving my car down its one main street
past colonnades of one-hundred-year-old oaks
dropping yellow leaves and the quaint shops

that have been closed for thirty years or more
and turned down a short abandoned street
I had long set my course away from in the past,

with its one white Victorian house, paint flaking,
the quiet held beneath its screened-in front porch,
someone's voice whispering: you can't go home.

My brother recently bought the house
we grew up in after moving back here
to a sleepy little town I left for the city,
but riding this same stretch of highway,
a strong fidelity, a feeling I can't shake,
whelms up in me when I see the fields
frosted with snow, snowmobile tracks
leading away into a treeline to places
unreachable by roads. The amplitude
of other times, a hermit's inheritance,
emerging out of the swirl and solitude.
I turn onto a road that bears my name
and that of a saint, patron of travellers,
watching the world shift, half-expecting,
to see my life and times at one remove
as if all this snow would stop its falling
a moment in mid-air, and I would see
my younger self walking away from me
like a sad child lost inside a fairy tale
vanishing into woods thick with wolves.
Or perhaps more like a Bruegel painting
where beyond the high church steeples,
black smoke rising from little chimneys,
peasants skating in small arrangements
on the ice of a deep imponderable lake,
there is a man and his boy trekking up
a ridge towards the forest's hinterlands
where a cabin awaits them in the hills,
its fire blazing in the cold winter nights.
I turn my car into the drive of a house
thinking "a blood-stained spirit has no
home," as Tu Fu once put it, knowing

the old house my brother and I shared
burned down under the weight of a fire.
My brother greets me at his front door,
then takes me down to look at a pantry
once my room, empty of my possessions,
so the life I always imagined for myself,
a small town regular in a deserted tavern,
that feeling of *saudade* is burned away too
by time's passage. I talk with my brother
until old patterns of stars begin emerging
like galaxies à la carte so I might believe
my younger self made it back to his home,
the lights still on in the recollecting dark,
the child in the nursery tale made it out
of the forest unhurt by packs of wolves,
and the woodsman and his young son,
after trekking the many miles across hills
and valleys, followed these illegible stars,
fixed points of light, all they understand
of heaven, to the small cabin in the trees
awaiting their return, the snow collecting
in their footprints so any trace of them
passing that way will be erased by dawn.

Dust

•

Today is my birthday while yesterday
the wind called to me as a boy asleep
in the branches of a crabapple tree,

whetted my sadness into a bitterness
after I cut my heart on the high seas
to find there was not a stable of gold

between my lips and a girl's oath was
a false promise banishing me to a city
covered in dust carried across the sea

from sand basins in the Gobi Desert.
Children wore surgical masks outside
while the tired and the old wiped grit

from their eyes like sleep. It covered
windows, neon signs, street vendors.
It was an ancient city sired by dreams.

Now that city and time are far away
and I find myself turned middle-aged
where death is no longer a dark wish

but a fine smattering of dust covering
every clear word I have ever fathomed.
Even the pockets in my clothes are full

of the smallest grains of my childhood,
the places I lived and the people's faces,
the memories of old times like syllables

rubbed together till nothing is left of me
but spent moments lifted into the wind
waiting to be carried far across the sea.

My Friends

·

We talked the whole night
about a poetry of longing.
How it dogs us at our heels
creating order from chaos,
leaving us all vulnerable
to move among mysteries
but penniless, long suffering,
unable to return the gift,
if that is what it is, after it takes
from us its pound of flesh,
places it upon a polished scale
and measures our labour
against the baffled silences
of the dead who learned
long ago to stay quiet.

The Old Life

•

The past comes back to us as a grail of loss,
as birdsong, old photographs, an empty sky.
Sometimes we hear it as thunder rolling above
the highways we walked along in the wilderness
of our youth. Often, thinking of the past means
entering each thought and building there a palace
in the present: be it an old life, a child's asylum,
or a maze of fictions. How faithful it is to keep
coming back to us, year after year. Our memories
forged in the golden crucible of its deep song.

In Asian folklore cranes symbolize longevity, immortality, and good fortune.

Herculaneum was a prosperous Roman town that was buried by the eruption of Mt. Vesuvius in 79 A.D. The Villa of the Papyri was the seaside home of Lucius Calpurnius Piso, whose magnificent library of scrolls is the only one to survive intact from antiquity.

Le Griffon was the vessel of French explorer René-Robert Cavelier, Sieur de La Salle. It is thought to have sunk in Northern Michigan but its final resting place has so far eluded underwater treasure hunters for centuries.

The first line of "Beginning Autumn" is the first line of a poem written by Robert Hass entitled "Songs to Survive the Summer" from his book *Praise*. (New York: Ecco, 1979.)

Moonrise, Hernandez is an iconic photograph taken by the American photographer Ansel Adams in 1941. I took liberties with the story of its creation by not including Cedric Wright who was also in Ansel's old Pontiac station wagon on that important evening.

Django Reinhardt was a pioneering Jazz guitarist. The *Porajmos* refers to the Nazi regime's mass murder of European gypsies. I borrowed a few words and phrases from a biography by Alain Antonietto which appeared as part of a ten CD boxset *Djangology* (EMI France)

The Portuguese word *saudade* is a feeling of improbable yearning. In an essay entitled "Boston and Kingsley," Jim Harrison explains the term as "a home-sickness for a home that never quite existed.

Poems from this manuscript were selected for the CBC Literary Awards shortlist in 2008. I am grateful to the Ontario Arts Council who provided me with a works-in-progress grant that enabled me to complete this manuscript; to Adam Getty, Christian Thompson and Paul Vermeersch who were the first readers of these poems; also thanks to Michael Holmes for his patience and editorial acumen; to Rob Winger for a crackerjack copyedit; and finally, grateful acknowledgement is made to the editors of *Arc Poetry Magazine*, *Event*, *Maple Tree Literary Supplement* and the *Malahat Review*.